GRAN CANARIA TRAVEL GUIDE 2024

Discovering the Island's Rich History and Heritage

DANIEL L. PORTER

Gran Canaria Travel Guide 2024

All Right Reserved!

No Part of this book may be reproduced, stored in a retrieval system, or transmitted in any form or by any means, electronic or mechanical, photocopying, recording or otherwise, without the prior written permission of the copyright owner

Copyright ©Daniel L. Porter, 2024.

Gran Canaria Travel Guide 2024

TABLE OF CONTENTS

INTRODUCTION

GRAN CANARIA ESSENTIALS

PLANNING YOUR TRIP

EXPLORING GRAN CANARIA

OUTDOOR ACTIVITIES

CULTURE AND HERITAGE

FOOD AND DRINK

SHOPPING

FAMILY TRAVEL

DAY TRIPS AND EXCURSIONS

BUSINESS AND CONFERENCES

SPECIAL INTEREST TRAVEL

GRAN CANARIA ON A BUDGET

NEW UPDATES AND EXPECTATIONS IN GRAN CANARIA FOR 2024

LOCAL INSIGHTS

CONCLUSION

FREQUENTLY ASKED QUESTIONS

Gran Canaria Travel Guide 2024

INTRODUCTION

With plenty to offer every kind of tourist, **Gran Canaria is a bustling and diversified destination tucked away in the heart of the Canary Islands.** This island paradise offers it everything, whether you're looking for sun-drenched beaches, thrilling outdoor pursuits, deep cultural experiences, or delectable food.

We'll take you on a tour around Gran Canaria's captivating scenery and vibrant villages with this all-inclusive travel guide Every part of the island has its distinct appeal and charms, from the calm mountain villages to the busy capital city of Las Palmas de Gran Canaria. This book is intended to be your go-to resource when organizing your trip to Gran Canaria.

Important details like **when to go, what to see, how to get there, what to bring, and how to behave while traveling are all included.** We have everything you need, whether you're a frugal tourist seeking for inexpensive lodging or a luxury seeker looking for excellent eating and upmarket activities. Come along as we discover off-the-beaten-path hidden treasures, taste delectable Canarian food, and learn about the history and culture of Gran Canaria.

Whatever your trip plans—**solo, family**- or group-oriented Gran Canaria guarantees life-changing events and treasured memories. So gather your belongings, fasten your seatbelt and get ready for an incredible journey to **Gran Canaria!**

About This Guide

Whether you're an experienced traveler or a first-time visitor, you can discover all the information you need about the island's culinary choices, lodgings, and activities here. You'll find thorough explanations of Gran Canaria's best attractions, helpful advice for organizing your vacation, and suggestions for experiences and activities catered to each trav-eler's interests and price range.

How to Utilize This Manual

This book is divided into simple parts to make your navigation of Gran Canaria a breeze. To obtain information on particular themes, such as organizing your vacation, seeing the island, engaging in outdoor activities, getting to know the local way of life and more, just turn the pages or consult the table of contents. You will find plenty of insightful information, insider knowledge, and suggestions in each area to assist you in planning the perfect itinerary for **Gran Canaria**. You may discover all the information you want here, whether your interests lie in exploring the island's rich history and culture, doing outdoor excursions, or just unwinding on immaculate beaches

A Quick Look at Gran Canaria

Gran Canaria is a vibrant, varied vacation spot that has something to offer everyone. **This Spanish island**, which lies off the coast of Africa in the Atlantic Ocean, has a year-round pleasant temperature that makes it a great destination for both outdoor lovers and sun worshippers. Discover the abundance of experiences that Gran Canaria has to offer, ranging from the lively streets of Las Palmas de Gran Canaria, the island's major city, to the serene towns tucked away in the mountains. Discover fascinating historical sites, savor delectable Canarian cuisine, relax on beautiful beaches, go on exhilarating outdoor excursions, and soak up the sun.

Whatever your reason for visiting Gran Canaria, its breathtaking scenery, lively culture, and kind people will charm you. **Please feel free to contact any of the listed businesses directly by email or through their official websites if you have any particular reservations or questions about the sights, lodging or activities that are included in this book.** you guarantee your position and get the best offers, be sure you book early since prices may fluctuate based on the season and availability.

GRAN CANARIA ESSENTIALS

Gran Canaria provides visitors with a wide range of experiences because of its varied landscapes and vibrant culture. Knowing the musts for traveling to this island paradise is vital for an amazing vacation, regardless of your travel goals unwinding on immaculate beaches, experiencing adventure in the highlands, or being fully immersed in the native way of life.

Best Times to Visit

Gran Canaria is a popular holiday destination for those looking for warmth and sunlight because of its year-round temperate temperature. The ideal time to go, however, will depend on your tastes and objectives.

Summer (June to August): With temperatures between **25°C and 30°C,** this season is perfect for beachgoers and fans of water sports. Since it's the busiest travel season, crowded beaches and more expensive lodging are to be expected.

Spring (March to May) and Autumn (September to November) These shoulder seasons are ideal for outdoor activities like trekking and seeing the island's natural beauties since they provide nice weather and less congestion.

Winter (December to February): Gran Canaria has lots of sunlight despite the lower temperatures, which range from **18 to 22 degrees Celsius.** Winter is the best season for tourists to visit warmer places and take in the laid-back vibe.

The Top 7 Standouts

Discover Las Palmas de Gran Canaria, the lively capital city with its enticing markets, ancient buildings, and cultural attractions.

Dunes of Maspalomas: Take a walk or take a camel ride atop these breathtaking dunes that elongate the southern shore.

Roque Nublo: Take a hike to this well-known volcanic rock formation for sweeping views of the untamed terrain of the island.Puerto de Mogán: Take a stroll around the quaint fishing hamlet, sometimes referred to as **"Little Venice"** because of its vibrant architecture and scenic canals.

Tejeda: Discover this charming mountain community, renowned for its traditional architecture and breathtaking vistas, tucked away in the volcanic interior of Gran Canaria.

Agaete: Unwind in Las Salinas' natural pools or stroll around the charming alleys of this seaside community, which is well-known for its coffee farms and tropical fruits.

Dorado Beach: Take advantage of a day at one of Gran Canaria's stunning beaches with golden sand for swimming and tanning.

Cueva Pintada Museum: Travel back in time and discover the history of Canaria, the island's native people, via the exhibit of archeological items and cave paintings.

Palmitos Park: This family-friendly destination tucked up in the highlands offers a wealth of floral gardens and unique species. Hike down the gorgeous valley of Barranco de Guayadeque to discover the raw beauty of Gran Canaria's interior, which is home to cave houses and traditional Canarian cuisine.

Gran Canaria Itineraries

There is an itinerary to fit any traveler's interests, regardless of how long you have to spend exploring Gran Canaria: a few days or a few weeks. Listed below are some recommended itineraries to help you maximize your time on the island.

Weekend Getaway: Take a day excursion to the charming towns of Agaete and Tejeda, explore Las Palmas de Gran Canaria, and unwind on Maspalomas beaches.

One-Week Adventure: Take a few days to hike through the mountains, see the parks, and see historical places like Roque Nublo and the Cueva Pintada Museum.

Beach Vacation: Take time to enjoy water sports and beachfront restaurants while lounging on the beautiful beaches of Playa del Inglés, Puerto Rico, and Puerto de.

Mogán.Packing Advice

Lightweight apparel appropriate for warm climatesBeach towels and swimwearSunscreen and eyewear comfortable walking shoes for sightseeing sun protection, use a cap or hat. A daypack for excursions and trekking European plug adaptor for travel.

Travel Tips and Etiquette

To converse with people in the area, pick up a few simple Spanish words.

Observe regional traditions and customs, including clothing regulations at places of worship. Keep hydrated by carrying a reusable water container, particularly while engaging in outdoor activities. In restaurants, leave a tip of around 10% if the bill does not include service. Pay attention to your surroundings and possessions, particularly in popular tourist destinations.

Safety and Health

Make sure you have emergency medical coverage and adequate travel insurance. To avoid becoming sick from the heat, drink plenty of water and use sunscreen. Observe safety precautions while engaging in outdoor pursuits such as hiking and water sports. In busy tourist places, stay on the lookout for pickpockets and make sure your possessions are safe. In an emergency, contact 112 to get help right away.

Contacts for Emergencies

Emergency services: 112 (fire, ambulance, and police). Police for tourists: **+34 928 219 21**

Emergency medical cases: 061 Support from consulates (for foreign nationals): Speak with your consulate or embassy. By remembering these necessities, you'll be ready to take advantage of all **Gran Canaria has to offer and guarantee a secure and enjoyable trip**.

PLANNING YOUR TRIP

When organizing a vacation to Gran Canaria, there are several things to take into account, such as lodging, travel insurance, and budgeting and transportation. This is a thorough guide to help you organize the ideal vacation to this charming island.

Planning Your Trip's Budget

To make sure you can enjoy Gran Canaria to the fullest without going over budget, make a plan for your trip before you go. When you are preparing your budget, take into account things like lodging, transportation, food, entertainment, and memento purchases. It will be easier for you to budget your money and determine how much you'll need for your vacation if you look up typical costs for different items.

Gran Canaria Airport (LPA) is the primary air entry point to the island, making it conveniently accessible by air. Direct flights from major cities in Europe and other areas of the globe are provided by several carriers. As an alternative, you may travel from mainland Spain or other Canary Islands to Gran Canaria by ferry. To guarantee the best rates and schedules for your trip dates, be sure to reserve your transportation well in advance.

Island Transportation

There are several ways to get about Gran Canaria once you are there to take in all of the varied sights the island has to offer.

Public Transportation: Global operates a dependable bus network in Gran Canaria that provides easy access to the island's main municipalities and popular tourist destinations. The majority of the island is served by bus lines, making them an economical and effective mode of transportation.

Car Rentals: For those who want to have the flexibility to see Gran Canaria at their speed, renting a car is a popular choice. Numerous car-rental agencies are present at the airport and popular tourist destinations, providing a selection of automobiles to fit your requirements and price range.

Taxis and ride-sharing: Taxis are a handy form of transportation for short excursions and are widely accessible in metropolitan areas and popular tourist destinations. In some areas of the island, ride-sharing services such as Uber are accessible and serve as a substitute for conventional taxi services.

Accommodations

A wide variety of lodging alternatives are available in Gran Canaria to accommodate the tastes and budgets of all visitors.

Hotels: Gran Canaria offers a variety of lodging options, ranging from opulent beachfront resorts to reasonably priced boutique hotels. You will have no trouble finding accommodations that meet your preferences, whether you're looking for a quaint bed & breakfast or all-inclusive luxuries.

Hostels: Providing inexpensive dorm-style lodging with shared amenities, hostels are the perfect choice for tourists on a tight budget or backpackers. For those who would like a little more luxury and solitude, several hostels also offer private rooms.

Holiday Rentals: When visiting Gran Canaria, think about renting a holiday house or apartment for a more individualized and homey experience. A wide range of rental accommodations, from roomy villas with views of the seaside to charming flats in the city, are available on websites like Airbnb.

Camping and Glamping

In approved locations, nature enthusiasts may fully immerse themselves in Gran Canaria's breathtaking surroundings. There are beautiful campgrounds and glamping spots all across the island, whether you like rustic camping beneath the stars or opulent camping with all the conveniences of home.

Travel Insurance: To safeguard yourself against unforeseen circumstances and crises, you must get travel insurance before departing on your journey to Gran Canaria. Medical costs, trip cancellations, lost or stolen property, and other unanticipated events may all be covered by travel insurance. Make sure your travel insurance policy satisfies your requirements and offers sufficient coverage for your trip by carefully going over its terms and alternatives for coverage.

You'll be ready to go on an amazing journey in Gran Canaria if you **properly plan and budget for your vacation**, reserve your lodging and transportation, and acquire travel insurance.

17

EXPLORING GRAN CANARIA

Discover Gran Canaria, a treasure trove of stunning landscapes, enthralling history, and vibrant culture. On the island, visitors may take advantage of a range of experiences, including the lively Las Palmas de Gran Canaria streets, serene mountain communities, and breathtaking beaches. Together, let's go on an excursion to discover the highlights of each Gran Canaria region.

Las Palmas, Gran Canaria

The vibrant metropolis of Las Palmas de Gran Canaria, the capital of Gran Canaria, is rich in attractions, culture, and history.

History and Culture: Explore the city's historic neighborhoods of Triana and Vegueta to see examples of its well-preserved colonial architecture. The renowned Santa Ana Cathedral and the Casa de Colón, a museum honoring Christopher Columbus, are located in these regions.

Communities: Wander through the charming streets of Vegueta, the city's oldest district, which is dotted with small businesses, cafés, and art galleries. Discover Triana's colorful boulevards, which are lined with restaurants, shops, and street performers.

Principal Attractions: Not to be missed are the Casa de Colón, the Museo Canario, and the Alfredo Kraus Auditorium, which hosts plays and other cultural events throughout the year.

Shopping and Markets: The bustling Triana and Mesa y López shopping districts are a great place to indulge in some retail therapy. These regions are home to a range of luxury boutiques, department stores, and local businesses that sell homemade goods and souvenirs. Don't miss the Mercado de Vegueta for fresh veggies, artisan items, and locally prepared meals.

Dining & Nightlife: Enjoy Canarian specialties as well as foreign cuisine and fresh seafood at one of the many restaurants in Las Palmas de Gran Canaria's flourishing restaurant scenes. For an exciting evening of dancing, go to the lively pubs and clubs in the Puerto de la Luz district after dark.

North Coast

Take in the rugged beauty of Gran Canaria's North Coast, which is dotted with charming towns, significant historical sites, and magnificent natural surroundings.

Agaete and Puerto de las Nieves: After seeing the quaint village of Agaete, which is well-known for its natural pools and hot springs, go to Puerto de las Nieves' picturesque harbor to indulge in fresh seafood and enjoy the breathtaking views of the surrounding sea.

Gáldar and Painted Cave: Explore the breathtaking Cueva Pintada (Painted Cave), a UNESCO World Heritage Site including archeological artifacts and ancient Canarian cave paintings. Gáldar is a settlement from antiquity.

Firgas and Waterfall Route: Drive slowly through the little town of Firgas, which is well-known for its lush surroundings and cascading waterfalls. Firgas and Waterfall Route. It is strongly suggested to hike the Waterfall Route, which winds through the neighboring mountains and provides stunning views of the island's interior.

East Coast

Discover the unknown gems of Gran Canaria's East Coast, which offers thrilling water sports spots in addition to historic towns and cultural landmarks.

Telde: Discover Telde, a medieval village known for its well-kept colonial structures and ancient Guanche tunnels. Discover the charming lanes of the historic district and pay a visit to the Basilica of San Juan Bautista, one of the oldest churches in the Canary Islands .

Ingenio: Learn about Ingenio, an agricultural hamlet renowned for its handicrafts and sugar cane fields. Visit the Museo de la Caña y El Azúcar to learn about the island's sugar cane industry, or stop by the Casa del Reloj, a historic house turned cultural center.

Pozo Izquierdo: One of the best places in the world to windsurf en Pozo Izquierdo, a beach community. Due to its ideal conditions and powerful winds, Pozo Izquierdo is a well-liked location for windsurfers and kiteboarders from all over the globe.

South Coast

Explore the sunny beaches and lively resort areas of Gran Canaria's South Coast, where fun and relaxation are just waiting to be experienced.

Maspalomas and Playa del Inglés: Enjoy a stroll over the well-known dunes or rest on Maspalomas Beach's beautiful beaches. The nearby town of Playa del Inglés has a thriving nightlife, great shopping, and thrilling entertainment.

Discover Puerto Rico and Amadores: Learn about Puerto Rico, a fun family getaway location renowned for its variety of water activities and protected beaches. In addition to having beautiful views of the Atlantic Ocean and crystal-clear waves, the quiet Amadores beach lies nearby.

Mogán and Puerto de Mogán: Wander about the charming fishing village of Mogán, known as the "Venice of the Canary Islands" because of its charming canals and bridges. Discover the bustling port of Puerto de Mogán, which is populated by a lively market, seafood eateries, and a waterfront promenade.

West Coast

Discover Gran Canaria's beautiful West Coast, which is dotted with quaint towns, breathtaking landscapes, and hidden jewels. Explore this location by deviating from the usual path.

La Aldea de San Nicolás: Discover the remote village of La Aldea de San Nicolás, which is encircled by mountains and nestled in a lush valley. Explore the town's historic church, stroll around its charming streets, and eat at local restaurants that provide real Canarian cuisine.

Tasarte & Tasartico: To escape the crowd and re-establish a connection with nature, stop by the tranquil villages of Tasarte and Tasartico. Enjoy the peace of this remote location by visiting unexplored beaches, trekking through wild mountains, and other activities.

Central Mountains

See the breathtaking landscape, historical buildings, and expansive views as you go into the heart of Gran Canaria's Central Mountains.

Pico de las Nieves: Ascend Pico de las Nieves, the highest peak on the island, for expansive vistas of the surrounding islands and Gran Canaria's diverse terrain. On a clear day, you may even be able to glimpse Mount Teide in neighboring Tenerife.

Roque Nublo: Hike to Roque Nublo, a well-known rock formation that symbolizes Gran Canaria's natural beauty and serves as a sacred site for the island's indigenous Guanche people. Enjoy sweeping views of the island's volcanic scenery from this fantastic vantage point.

Tejeda and Artenara: Explore these charming mountain villages, known for their exquisite handicrafts, traditional Canarian architecture, and breathtaking views. See the Gran Canaria Ethnographic Museum in Tejeda to learn more about the traditions and agricultural past of the island.

Whether you're drawn to the lively energy of Las Palmas de Gran Canaria, the wild beauty of the North Coast, the sun-drenched beaches of the South Coast, or the tranquil villages of the **West Coast and Central Mountains, exploring Gran Canaria promises incredible experiences and breathtaking scenery at every turn.**

OUTDOOR ACTIVITIES

Gran Canaria is a haven for nature lovers, providing a wide variety of outdoor pursuits that capitalize on the island's distinctive topography and temperate environment. The island's natural splendor, which includes sun-kissed beaches, untamed mountains, and lush woods, makes it the ideal setting for both adventure and leisure. This is a comprehensive guide to Gran Canaria's outdoor activities.

Seashores Top Beaches

Las Canteras Beach

Stretching over three kilometers, this urban beach in Las Palmas is among the nicest in all of Europe. With a bustling promenade with shops, cafés, and restaurants, it's ideal for swimming, snorkeling, and sunbathing.

Maspalomas: This gorgeous length of golden sand beach is well-known for its enormous dunes. It's perfect for strolling among the dunes, sunbathing, and camel rides.Playa del Inglés: Known for its lively environment, water sports, and nightlife, this beach is close to Maspalomas. It's a well-liked location for adventure and leisure.

Playa de Amadores: Amadores Beach is a great place to spend a leisurely day by the sea because of its serene, blue seas and family-friendly vibe. Excellent beach amenities include restaurants along the waterfront, sun lounges, and umbrellas.

Playa de Güigüi: On the west coast, Güigüi Beach provides peace and undisturbed natural beauty for a more private experience. Reachable by boat or an arduous climb, it's a secret treasure for those in search of seclusion.Water Activities:

Surfing: Gran Canaria is a top choice for surfers of all skill levels due to its reliable waves and plenty of surf schools. Playa de Las Canteras, El Confital, and Playa del Inglés are a few of the well-known locations.

Windsurfing and Kitesurfing: Because of the great wind and conditions, Pozo Izquierdo on the east coast is a well-known location for windsurfing and kitesurfing.

Snorkeling and diving: The island is a great place to go snorkeling and diving because of its crystal-clear seas and abundant marine life. Sardina del Norte and El Cabrón Marine Reserve are well-liked diving locations.

Stand-Up Paddleboarding (SUP): An enjoyable method to explore the coastline, SUP is best enjoyed in the calm seas around beaches like Amadores and Anfi del Mar.Trails for

Walking and Hiking Easy Trails

Barranco de los Cernícalos: This picturesque route near Telde winds through a verdant gorge and leads to many lovely waterfalls. Families may enjoy this somewhat simple climb.

Mirador de la Degollada de las Yeguas: A quick and simple stroll leads to a viewpoint with breathtaking views of the surrounding countryside and the Fataga ravine.

Trails for Intermediates: Roque Nublo, A modest climb leading to one of Gran Canaria's most famous sites. The hike takes one to two hours to complete and gives breathtaking vistas of the island's untamed interior.

Caldera de Bandama: This walk circles the edge of an old volcanic crater and provides expansive views over the island's middle section. The trek takes two to three hours and is somewhat difficult.

Trails for Experts: Pico de las Nieves: Offering stunning views and a strenuous journey across a variety of terrains, this island's highest summit is ideal for experienced hikers. The Camino de Santiago is a long-distance hiking path that crosses the island from Maspalomas to Gáldar. It is strenuous yet rewarding for experienced walkers.

Routes for Cycling Road Cycling

Take in the breathtaking views as you cycle along the coast of Gran Canaria. Some routes link well-known beach communities like Playa del Inglés, Maspalomas, and Puerto de Mogán. These routes include generally flat terrain and magnificent views of the ocean

Mountain Routes: Cycle across the middle mountains for a more strenuous ride. Steep climbs and thrilling descents may be found on routes like the loop around Roque Nublo or the climb to Pico de las Nieves, which reward you with expansive views.

La Cumbre mountain biking: Take a ride through pine woods, lava formations, and isolated communities as you explore the difficult routes in this area. There is a combination of picturesque fire roads and challenging singletrack in the region.Tamadaba Natural Park has a network of mountain bike-friendly trails that range in difficulty from beginner to expert. The paths provide breathtaking views of the island's west coast as they travel through thick woods.

AthleticsRock Climbing

The volcanic rock formations of Gran Canaria provide great chances for rock climbing. Ayacata, Sorrueda, and Fataga are well-known climbing locations with routes suitable for climbers of all abilities. For individuals who are new to the activity, there are climbing schools and guides available.Enjoy the exhilaration of paragliding over the breathtaking scenery of Gran Canaria. The cliffs of Los Giles and the mountains close to Ingenio are popular take-off locations because they provide amazing aerial views of the island's interior and coastline.

Snorkeling and diving: Gran Canaria is a popular snorkeling and diving destination because of its pristine seas and variety of marine life. Visit locations like Sardina del Norte and El Cabrón Marine Reserve to discover underwater caverns, shipwrecks, and colorful reefs. For all skill levels, there are dive facilities throughout the island that provide instruction and guided dives.

National Parks and Reserves for Nature and Wildlife

Tamadaba Natural Park is a park with stunning cliffs, deep ravines, and thick pine woods on the northwest coast. With well-marked routes and spectacular overlooks, it's a sanctuary for hikers and wildlife lovers.

Pilancones Natural Park: Located in the southern region of the island, Pilancones has a variety of flora and wildlife together with rough terrain. The park offers great chances for trekking and birding, and it is home to unique species.

Flora and Fauna: A wide variety of plant and animal life is supported by the many climates and ecosystems of Gran Canaria. Species like the Canary Island pine and laurel trees may be found in the island's woodlands. Native species found on the island include the gigantic lizard and the Gran Canaria blue chaffinch. Numerous fish species, dolphins, and sea turtles may all be found in coastal regions and marine parks.

Discovering Gran Canaria's outdoor activities provides many chances for exploration, leisure, and natural connection. There is something for every outdoor enthusiast to enjoy on the island, whether they are attracted to the breathtaking beaches, strenuous hiking paths, **picturesque cycling routes, or exhilarating adventure sports.**

CULTURE AND HERITAGE

Gran Canaria is a historical, cultural, and traditional melting pot influenced by modernity, colonialism, and indigenous heritage. The island's architecture, museums, festivals, music, dance, and language all showcase its rich cultural legacy.

History of Gran Canaria

The history of Gran Canaria is intriguing and goes back thousands of years. Originally hailing from North Africa, the Guanches were an indigenous Berber-speaking tribe that lived on the island. These first inhabitants constructed amazing stone constructions, many of which are still standing, and lived in cave shelters.

A major turning point in the **history of Gran Canaria was the Spanish invasion conducted by Juan Rejón in the late 15th century.** After the island was annexed by Castile, the Spanish started to have an impact on its society, culture, and architecture. After its founding in 1478, Las Palmas de Gran Canaria developed into a major center for exploration and commerce. Gran Canaria became a multicultural hub throughout the ages as a result of the impact of other civilizations, particularly British, Portuguese, and Dutch commerce.

The island's ancient towns, historical sites, and cultural customs all serve as reminders of its rich past.

Architecture

Reflecting the island's many cultural influences, Gran Canaria's architecture combines colonial, Canarian, and contemporary architectural elements.Canarian traditional homes: "**Casas terreras,**" or traditional Canarian homes, are distinguished by their straightforward but endearing architecture. These homes usually have red-tiled roofs, sturdy walls made of stone or adobe, and wooden balconies. The **"patio canario,"** a central courtyard that acts as the home's heart and is often adorned with flowers and plants, is one of its most characteristic features. These homes may be seen in the old parts of cities like Tejeda in the central highlands and Vegueta near Las Palmas.

Older Structures and Landmarks

One of the most significant religious sites on the island is the church of Santa Ana, an outstanding Gothic church situated in the center of Vegueta, Las Palmas. A variety of architectural styles are the consequence of its multi-century construction, which started in the 15th century and took several centuries to finish. The ancient Casa de Colón, located near Vegueta, is said to have been visited by Christopher Columbus during his explorations of the New World. It now contains a museum devoted to the history of the Canary Islands and the explorers.

Pueblo Canario: This cultural complex, which is located in Las Palmas, has Canarian buildings in its original style and hosts folk dance and music events

Galleries and Museums

There are a plethora of museums and galleries on Gran Canaria that provide information about the island's history, art, and culture.

Museo Canario: Dedicated to the pre-Hispanic history of the Canary Islands, this museum is situated in Vegueta. It is home to a sizable collection of mummies, tools, and ceramics among other Guanche relics. In addition to examining Christopher Columbus's relationship to the Canary Islands, Casa de Colón is a museum that showcases the island's nautical and colonial past.

CAAM, or Centro Atlántico de Arte Moderno, is a museum of contemporary art featuring artwork by artists from Latin America, Spain, and the Canary Islands. It is located in Vegeta's old area.

Museo Elder de la Ciencia y la Tecnología: This interactive science and technology museum is ideal for families and has hands-on displays on a variety of scientific themes. It is located in the Santa Catalina Park neighborhood of Las Palmas.

Festivals and Events

From boisterous carnivals to traditional religious festivals, Gran Canaria's festivals and events are a dynamic representation of its cultural past.

Annual Festival: The Carnival of Las Palmas de Gran Canaria, which takes place in February and includes parades, music, dancing, and extravagant costumes, is one of the most well-known and vibrant festivals on the island. The Carnival Parade and the Drag Queen Gala are the two primary events.

Fiesta de San Juan: Held in June, this celebration honors both the summer solstice and the establishment of Las

Palmas. Cultural performances, pyrotechnics, and bonfires are also part of the celebrations.

Fiesta del Almendro en Flor: This Tejeda, California, celebration of traditional music, dancing, and regional food takes place in **January and February to honor the almond blossom season.**

Regional Holidays: Romerías are customary pilgrimages that take place in different communities around the island. The residents dress in traditional Canarian clothing, lead processions to a nearby church, and celebrate with eating, dancing, and folk music. Día de Canarias: **Held on May 30th,** this official holiday honors the Canary Islands' independence. activities showcasing Canarian crafts and food, traditional music, dance performances, and cultural activities commemorate the day.

Dance and Music

Gran Canaria's culture is strongly reflected in its dance and music, which combine contemporary and traditional elements in a seamless whole.Folk Music: Known as **"folklore,"** traditional Canarian music is played on instruments such as the temple, a little instrument

36

resembling a guitar, guitar, and drums. The "**isa,**" "**folía,**" and "**tajaraste**" are popular folk dances that are often done during regional celebrations and festivals.

Modern Music: From pop and rock to reggaeton and electronic music, the island has a thriving modern music scene. Throughout the year, Las Palmas is home to several music events that draw performers from both domestic and foreign markets.

Dialects and Languages Spanish

More especially the Canarian Spanish dialect, which has unique phonetic and lexical characteristics affected by its historical and geographic setting, is the official language of Gran Canaria.Pronunciation: Certain consonants, such as **"s" and "z,"** are pronounced softer in Canarian Spanish and are often aspirated or dropped at the end of syllables. Another way to pronounce the "ch" sound is as **"sh."Vocabulary.**

The dialect reflects the island's broad cultural influences by including terms from Portuguese, African, and the indigenous Guanche language.phrases: Canarian Spanish has certain unusual idioms and phrases that are not often used in mainland Spain. **"Guagua"** means **"bus,"** for instance, while **"fajarse"** implies **"to work hard."**

Gran Canaria's history, architecture, museums, festivals, music, dance, and language all reflect the island's rich cultural legacy. A fuller comprehension of the island's distinct personality and the dynamic energy of its inhabitants may be gained by investigating various facets of it. Gran Canaria's cultural tapestry is fascinating and enlightening, **whether you're having a traditional dinner, seeing historical sites, or going to a local festival.**

FOOD AND DRINK

Gran Canaria has a rich and varied food scene that matches its culture and background. The island's culinary culture offers something for every taste and price range, from sophisticated gourmet cuisine to traditional Canarian fare. An extensive overview of the food and beverages available in Gran Canaria is provided below.

Cuisine of the Canaries Must-Try Recipes

Papas Arrugadas are little, wrinkly potatoes that are cooked in salt water and then served with green (mojo verde), which is prepared with parsley and cilantro, or red (mojo), which is made with paprika and red peppers. They are a traditional Canarian meal that you have to have. A classic Canarian stew consisting of shredded chicken or beef, potatoes, veggies, and chickpeas is called . This meal, which represents the island's rustic culinary heritage, is rich and substantial.

Sancocho Canario: Boiled potatoes, sweet potatoes, and mojo sauce are served with salted fish, often sea bass or . It's a family favorite and a favorite for special occasions. Gofio is a sort of flour prepared from roasted grains that is a staple in the Canary Islands. It is often added to soups and stews or consumed for breakfast with milk or honey.

Bienmesabe: A classic dessert consisting of **sugar, egg yolks, lemon zest, and crushed almonds.** It is often used as a filling for pastries or served with ice cream.Street Cuisine: Fish sticks, or churros de Pescado, are deep-fried and often served with a lemon slice and aioli sauce. They are a well-liked street food snack, particularly in the vicinity of the shore.Canarian sandwiches called bocadillos are usually made with regional ingredients including cheese, tomatoes, and chorizo. You may get bocadillos at several local markets and food stands.

Empanadas: A popular street cuisine, these flavorful pastries with meat, fish, or vegetable fillings are ideal for on-the-go meals.

Restaurants and Dining

This restaurant, which is well-known for its delicious seafood dishes and sophisticated ambiance, provides a wonderful dining experience together with breathtaking views of Las Canteras Beach. It is advised to make reservations. contact@restaurantelasrias.com via email

Fine Dining: This classy eatery by the seaside offers a range of gourmet meals with an emphasis on using local, fresh products. It's ideal for a special event or a romantic evening. Reservations@elsenador.com is where you may make them.

Casual Dining: La Marinera (Las Palmas): Known for its superb seafood meals served in a laid-back seaside atmosphere, La Marinera is a favorite destination for both residents and visitors. The seafood paella and grilled fish are highly recommended.

Casa Josefina (Agaete): This home-cooked Canarian cuisine is the specialty of this family-owned restaurant. Local favorites include the grilled octopus and goat stew. You may walk right in without a reservation, but it's best to come early to guarantee a table

Options for a Budget

El Rinconcito de Canarias (Las Palmas) A little restaurant with reasonably priced typical Canarian fare. You must try the ropa vieja and papas arrugadas.

Mercado del Puerto (Las Palmas): This market is a great location to try a wide range of reasonably priced regional cuisine, including fresh seafood and tapas. For tourists on a tight budget who want to try the local food, this is a terrific place to go.

Bars and Nightlife

There are plenty of alternatives for a dynamic evening in Gran Canaria, from noisy nightclubs to relaxed beach bars.

La Azotea de Benito (Las Palmas): A hip rooftop bar with a large assortment of beverages and breathtaking city views. It's a terrific place to meet people, both residents and visitors, and have a drink in the evening

El Faro Lounge Bar (Maspalomas): Known for its superb drinks and sophisticated atmosphere, this bar is situated next to the well-known Maspalomas Lighthouse. It's ideal for a laid-back evening with views of the ocean and live music.

Mundo Bar (Playa del Inglés): This well-known bar has dance floors, DJs, and themed evenings in an energetic environment. For those who want to check out the island's nightlife, this is the place to go. Wineries and Regional BeveragesGran Canaria's wine sector has become well-known for its premium wines, which are made from vines that flourish in the volcanic soil and distinct climate of the island.

Bodega Los Berrazales (Agaete): This family-owned winery provides tours and wine tastings of their top-notch selections. Discover the winemaking process, take a tour of the vineyards, and taste a selection of wines paired with regional cheeses and hams. You may reserve tours by sending an email to info@losberrazales.com.Bodega

Vega de Gáldar (Gáldar): This winery provides tastings and guided tours and is well-known for its award-winning wines. A stroll through the vineyards and a wine tasting in the exquisite wine cellar are included in the experience. It is advised to make reservations, which may be done at tours@vegadegalder.com.nearby breweriesCervecería Isla

Verde (La Aldea de San Nicolás): Utilizing resources from the area, this craft brewery crafts a variety of artisanal beers. In addition to taking tours and learning about the brewing process, visitors may partake in tastings. Send an email to info@islaverdebrewery.com to schedule a tour.

Jaira (Las Palmas): Known for its Canarian-inspired beer range, Jaira is another prominent artisan brewery on the island.

They have a taproom where you may spend a leisurely evening while trying out several sorts. With delicious traditional tastes and contemporary inspirations, Gran Canaria's culinary scene has something to suit every taste and budget.

The island offers a wide variety of food and drink alternatives, from street cuisine and must-try Canarian specialties to fine dining establishments and reasonably priced cafes. Enjoying a wine-tasting tour, dining at a fine dining establishment, or **taking in the exciting nightlife are just a few of the culinary experiences that Gran Canaria has to offer.**

SHOPPING

Gran Canaria is a shopping haven, with a variety of duty-free shops, boutiques, contemporary malls, and local markets. Gran Canaria has something for everyone, whether you're searching for distinctive trinkets, cutting-edge apparel, or regional crafts. This is a thorough guide to island shopping.

Regional Markets Mercado de Vegueta(Las Palmas)

This oldest and busiest market on the island is situated in Vegueta's historic neighborhood. It provides a colorful assortment of regional specialties, fresh food, and handmade crafts. Everything from Canarian cheeses and meats to jewelry and handcrafted ceramics may be found here. The market is a fantastic location to sample the local food and culture. **It is open Monday through Saturday.** Mercado del Puerto (Las Palmas): This market, which is **close to Las Canteras Beach**, has a mix of modern food courts and pubs with traditional vendors. It's a bustling place to have a drink, purchase fresh fish, and try local cuisine. The market is **open every day** and often has activities and live music in the evenings.

Mercado de San Mateo: This weekend market, which is held in the mountain village of San Mateo, is well-known for its fresh local food, which includes fruits, vegetables, and handcrafted goods. It's a terrific location to get handcrafted items including cheeses, breads, and jams as well as fresh supplies. **Both Saturdays and Sundays are when the market is open.**

Mercadillo de Teror: Located in the quaint village of Terror, this market is well-known for its handcrafted goods, traditional Canarian goods, and textiles from the area. It takes place every Sunday. It's a great location to explore the island's rich cultural legacy and purchase souvenirs. Both residents and visitors may be seen enjoying the vast range of products offered at the market, which includes handcrafted lace and organic honey.

Retail Stores and Boutiques Centro Comercial Las Arenas (Las Palmas)

Las Arenas is one of the island's biggest shopping centers, with a huge selection of both local and foreign brands. It has a movie theater, a lot of restaurants, and stores. The mall is well situated for a shopping binge followed by a trip to Las Canteras Beach because of its handy location.

El Muelle Shopping Center (Las Palmas): This contemporary mall, which is close to the harbor, has a range of stores, including electronics and high-street apparel. It also offers a variety of eating establishments and recreational spaces, such as a movie theater and a bowling alley.
El Muelle is a great place to go shopping casually or on a family outing.

Centro Comercial Atlantico (Vecindario): Known for its wide array of retailers, including both regional shops and well-known global names, this shopping center is situated in the municipality of Vecindario. In addition, it has a sizable supermarket, which makes it a handy location for daily necessities and shopping.

Boutiques in Meloneras: Visit the resort district of Meloneras for a more posh shopping experience. Numerous upscale businesses selling designer clothing, jewelry, and accessories can be found here. In addition, the region has opulent hotels and excellent dining establishments, creating an upscale shopping experience.

Souvenirs and Handicrafts

A distinctive and genuine memento is made from traditional Canarian pottery. Beautifully produced items may be found at specialist stores and local markets. Decorative bowls, plates, and figurines are popular goods that often have elaborate patterns and vivid colors.

Simple: Exclusive to the Canary Islands, the temple is a little instrument resembling a guitar. It's a great keepsake or present, particularly for music lovers. Throughout the island, artisan markets and record stores sell thimbles.

Aloe Vera Products: Superior aloe vera products are a specialty of Gran Canaria. Aloe vera products range greatly in availability from health supplements to skincare creams and are sold in stores and marketplaces. These goods are highly valued for their all-natural moisturizing and healing qualities.

Canarian Embroidery: The Canary Islands are known for their handcrafted lace and embroidered linens. Tablecloths, napkins, and apparel are some examples of these exquisite things; they often include fine stitching and elaborate designs. Local markets and artisan stores carry them.

Honey Rum, or Ron Miel: A Canary Island specialty, Ron Miel is a fragrant, sweet liquor brewed with honey and rum. It makes a wonderful memento to bring back and show off to loved ones. All across the island, booze shops and supermarkets carry it.

Duty-Free Purchasing Las Palmas Port

With its duty-free status, Las Palmas provides fantastic chances for duty-free shopping. There are several stores in the port area where you may purchase tax-free items including electronics, cosmetics, fragrances, and tobacco. It's the perfect location to buy premium goods in bulk for less money.

Gran Canaria Airport: Travelers may enjoy a convenient shopping experience at Gran Canaria Airport thanks to its duty-free stores. From designer perfumes and cosmetics to regional specialties and spirits, you may buy a variety of goods here. Before your travel, it's the ideal location to pick up last-minute presents or mementos.

Yumbo Centrum (Playa del Inglés): This place has a variety of duty-free stores in addition to being well-known for its entertainment and nightlife. A wide range of goods, including apparel, gadgets, and trinkets, are available at affordable costs. The center is a well-liked location for entertainment and shopping.

The English Court (Las Palmas): For those who are not EU citizens, this well-known Spanish department store brand provides duty-free shopping. El Corte Inglés in Las Palmas offers a large assortment of premium products, such as gourmet cuisine, gadgets, home goods, and clothing. It's a great location for a whole shopping experience.

Gran Canaria offers a wide range of **shopping experiences to suit every preference and budget, ranging from contemporary malls and upscale shops to vibrant local markets.** Whether you're looking for duty-free deals, trendy clothing, or traditional handicrafts, the island provides a distinctive and entertaining shopping experience.

Spend some time browsing the many stores and bringing home a memento of the **vibrant cultural past of Gran Canaria.**

FAMILY TRAVEL

With a plethora of family-friendly attractions and activities, Gran Canaria is an excellent place to take holidays with the whole family. **A comprehensive guide to help you organize a fantastic family vacation to Gran Canaria** is provided here, including everything from stunning beaches and thrilling theme parks to kid-friendly attractions and helpful travel advice.

Family-Friendly Activities

Family-Friendly EventsPalmitos Park is a great family attraction and is situated in the southern part of the island. Birds, reptiles, and mammals are among the exotic species on display at this botanical park and zoo. The parrot and dolphin displays are sure to delight kids, while the aquarium and butterfly house provide informative experiences. There are many picnic spaces and eateries in this well-kept park. Go to www.palmitos park.es, their website, for further information.

Poema del Mar Aquarium: This cutting-edge aquarium, which is located in Las Palmas, offers guests of all ages an immersive underwater experience. A vast variety of marine life, including enormous sharks and rays as well as vibrant tropical species, are on display at the aquarium. For kids, it's an entertaining and instructive visit with interactive exhibits and educational displays.

Check out www.poema-del-mar.com for information on tickets and hours of operation.

The biggest water park in Gran Canaria is called **Aqualand Maspalomas.** It has a variety of water slides, wave pools, and lazy rivers that are great for a fun-filled family day out. With sections of the park reserved for younger visitors, there's something fun and safe to do for everyone. Further details are available at www.aqualand.es/maspalomas.

Cocodrilo Park: A zoo and rescue facility in Agüimes, the park is home to a wide range of creatures, including birds, large cats, crocodiles, and monkeys. Through engaging activities like animal exhibitions and feeding sessions, the park helps kids learn about wildlife protection. Go to www.cocodriloparkzoo.com for further information.

Angry Birds Activity Park: This Puerto Rican theme park caters to younger kids with a variety of play areas, obstacle courses, and interactive activities that are based on the well-known **Angry Birds video game series.** It's a great spot where kids can run off steam and parents can unwind. Go to www.activityparkcanarias.com to learn more.

Top Beaches for Families Playa de Las Canteras (Las Palmas)

Known for its smooth sand, calm waves, and many amenities, Playa de Las Canteras is one of the island's most visited beaches. With plenty of area for kids to play and a promenade lined with eateries and cafés, the beach is perfect for families.

Playa de Amadores is a man-made beach with beautiful, golden sand and crystal-clear seas that is situated on the southwest coast. It's ideal for beginning swimmers because of the gradual incline and quiet waters. There are several food choices close by, as well as loungers and umbrellas at the beach.

Playa de Puerto Rico: This protected beach is well-known for its serene waves and welcoming environment for families. Everything you need for a day at the beach is close by in the form of stores and restaurants, and the neighboring marina provides chances for boat rides and water sports.

Playa de Mogán: The little village of Puerto de Mogán is home to the lovely beach known as Playa de Mogán. Children may play safely on this beach because of its shallow seas and strong protection. The neighborhood's stores, restaurants serving seafood, and attractive promenades make it ideal for a fun family day.

Attractions and Theme Parks

Holiday World Maspalomas is a family-friendly theme park situated in Maspalomas. In addition to a mini-golf course, bowling alley, and arcade games, it offers a range of attractions, such as bumper cars, roller coasters, and Ferris wheels. Along with a variety of food choices, the park often holds events and entertainment. Go to www.holidayworldmaspalomas.com for more details.Sioux

City Park: At Sioux City Park in San Bartolomé de Tirajana, take a trip back in time to the Wild West. This interactive theme park brings the Old West to life with live acts, reenactments, and shows. Youngsters may visit the sheriff's office, go on pony rides, and see exciting shootout demonstrations. Go to www.siouxcitypark.es for further information.Cactualdea Park is a remarkable botanical park with hundreds of species of cacti from all over the globe. It is situated near La Aldea de San Nicolás. A historic Canarian hamlet, replete with eateries and artisan stores, is also replicated in the park. Families may have an entertaining and instructive day out here. Go to www.cactualdea.com to learn more.

Tips for Traveling with Children

It's important to prepare ahead when traveling with kids. Lodging plan, look into family-friendly activities and make a flexible schedule that includes breaks and leisure. A well-planned itinerary can guarantee a stress-free travel experience.

Think Before You Pack: Don't forget to include sunscreen, caps, swimsuits, snacks, and any required prescriptions in your child's bag. Along with some entertainment for the kids (books, toys, or other gadgets), pack a tiny first aid kit.Select Family-Friendly Lodging:

Seek family-friendly hotels or vacation homes. Family rooms, kid-friendly amenities, swimming pools, and kids' clubs **are available at a lot of Gran Canaria lodgings**. To choose the finest solutions for your family's requirements, go through reviews and ratings.

Drink plenty of water and take care of the heat. Gran Canaria has a bright environment, so you'll need to shield your family from the sun. Make sure everyone wears sunscreen often and remains hydrated by encouraging them to drink plenty of water. To protect yourself from the sun's rays, dress in light clothes, caps, and sunglasses.Accept

Local Cuisine: Teach your kids to sample the cuisine and tastes of the area. A lot of Canarian food, such as grilled fish and papas , is kid-friendly. Learn about the menus in your area and find eateries that provide a range of choices to accommodate the preferences of all patrons.Use Public

Transportation: Getting about the island may be simpler with Gran Canaria's effective public transportation system, which includes buses and taxis. Strollers may be accommodated by buses, and taxis are often accessible. If you want to go at your leisure to more isolated locations, think about hiring a vehicle.

Take Part in Cultural Activities: Incorporate cultural activities into your vacation, including going to museums, seeing festivals in the area, or seeing historical places. Children may get a greater grasp of Gran Canaria's rich legacy via these engaging and informative activities.

Keep an Eye on Safety: Make sure your kids are under constant supervision at all times, particularly in busy places or near water. Instruct children on fundamental safety measures, such as staying put and knowing where to go for assistance in case they get lost. In case of any problems, familiarize yourself with medical facilities and emergency contacts.

To guarantee a wonderful family holiday, Gran Canaria has an abundance of family-friendly activities, stunning beaches, thrilling theme parks, and helpful travel advice. With careful preparation, thoughtful packing, and an embrace of the local way of life, **you and your kids may make enduring memories and have a stress-free vacation.**

DAY TRIPS AND EXCURSIONS

From touring neighboring islands to taking boat tours and guided experiences, **Gran Canaria** has an abundance of options for day trips and excursions that suit a range of interests. The top day outings and excursions from Gran Canaria are included in this thorough guide.

Adjacent Islands Tenerife

How to Get There: From Gran Canaria, Tenerife, the biggest of the Canary Islands, is readily accessible. From Las Palmas or Agaete, you may go to Santa Cruz de Tenerife via boat. It takes around **1.5 to 2 hours to go by boat. An alternative is to take a quick 30-minute trip from Gran Canaria Airport to Tenerife North or South Airport.**

Things to Look for and Take Action on:

Park Teide: This UNESCO World Heritage Site, which is home to Mount Teide, Spain's highest peak, provides breathtaking views of volcanic landscapes. Hiking through the park's distinctive landscape or taking a cable car trip to the close peak for breath-blowing vistas are two options.

The well-known animal park Loro Parque, which is situated near Puerto de la Cruz, is home to a diverse range of animals, such as marine life, parrots, and penguins. Families with children and animal lovers will appreciate this area.

Siam Park is a well-known water park in **Costa Adeje** that has wave pools, a lazy river, and exhilarating water slides. It is regarded as one of the world's top water parks. Discover Santa Cruz de Tenerife, the capital of the island renowned for its vivacious markets, ancient architecture, and rich culture. Don't overlook the stunning Plaza de España and the Auditorio de Tenerife.

Fuerteventura Arriving

Another fantastic island to explore from Gran Canaria is Fuerteventura, which is renowned for its breathtaking beaches and distinctive terrain. It takes two to three hours to go on the ferry from Las Palmas to Puerto del Rosario or Morro Jable. It takes around forty minutes for flights to go from Gran Canaria Airport to Fuerteventura Airport.Things to Look for and Take Action on Corralejo

60

Natural Park: This park has immaculate beaches and towering dunes. It's ideal for enjoying the beauty of nature, sandboarding, and tanning.Betancuria: A little town rich in history, Betancuria was formerly the capital of the island. Explore the charming streets and nearby museums while paying a visit to the Santa María Church.

Oasis Wildlife - Fort Lauderdale: This destination, which is a sizable zoo and botanical garden, provides up-close interactions with a range of animals and a lovely environment for a family day. Kite surfers and windsurfers will find heaven at Sotavento Beach, which is well-known for its golden dunes and crystal-clear waves.

Boat ExpeditionsWhale and Dolphin Watching

A variety of whale and dolphin species may be seen in the seas of Gran Canaria. Numerous businesses provide boat trips that leave Puerto Rico and Puerto de Mogán and take you out to sea to see these amazing animals in their environment. The trips usually last between two and three hours, and they often include refreshments and knowledgeable commentary on marine life.

Spirit of the Sea (www.dolphin whale.es) and Lineas Salmon (www.lineassalmon.com) are two trustworthy suppliers.

Catamaran Cruises: Take into consideration a catamaran cruise for a leisurely day on the sea. Along with food and beverages on board, these tours sometimes feature pauses at private bays for swimming and snorkeling. Anfi del Mar and Puerto Rico are popular places to live.

Packages from companies like Blue Spirit Catamaran (www.blue spirit catamaran.com) and Afrikat (www.afrikat.com) are available.

Glass-Bottom Boat trips: For families and people who want to learn about marine life without getting wet, these trips are great. Glass-bottom boats provide you with an unparalleled perspective of the undersea environment, letting you observe fish, corals, and other marine life. Numerous ports, notably Puerto de Mogán and Puerto Rico, provide these trips.Sunset Cruises: Sail away to see Gran Canaria's breathtaking sunsets. Sunset cruises, which often leave in the late afternoon, provide breathtaking views of the Atlantic Ocean as the sun sets.

Drinks and food are often provided on these cruises, making for a lovely and unforgettable evening. These cruises are provided by operators such as Blue Boat (www.blueboat.es) and Exclusive Boat (www.exclusive boat charters.com).

Tours with a Guide Gran Canaria Island Tour

Take a thorough guided tour to see the island's varied landscapes and rich cultural legacy. Important sites including the Bandama Caldera, the Roque Nublo, the ancient town of Terror, and the charming hamlet of Tejeda are often visited on these trips.

Several companies, such as Low-Cost Tours Gran Canaria (www.low cost tours gran canaria.com) and LCT Europe (www.lcteurope.com), are available for booking tours. Wine

Tasting Tours: Take a guided wine-tasting tour to learn about Gran Canaria's rich wine history. See regional vineyards in the island's north and center to taste a range of wines and learn about the winemaking process. Bodega Las Tirajanas in San Bartolomé de Tirajana and Bodega Los Berrazales in Agaete are often visited on tours. Well-known companies include Canary Wine Tours (www.canarywinetours.com) and GC Wine Tours (www.gc

wine-tours.com).Historical and Cultural Tours: Take a guided tour that highlights historical monuments and cultural locations to explore Gran Canaria's rich history and culture. The Casa de Colón, the Catedral de Santa Ana, and the quaint alleyways of Vegueta in Las Palmas are often visited on these trips. Examine trips offered by organizations such as Trip Gran Canaria (www.tripgrancanaria.com) and Urban Adventures (www.urban adventures.com).

Hiking & Nature trips: For those who like the great outdoors, guided hiking trips are a great way to see the natural beauty of Gran Canaria. You follow knowledgeable guides over beautiful routes in places like the central highlands, the Barranco de Guayadeque, and the Tamadaba Natural Park.

These excursions provide visitors with knowledge about the island's geology, vegetation, and animals. Numerous hiking excursions are available from companies like Walk In Gran Canaria (www.walkingrancanaria.com) and Rock Natour (www.rocknatour.com).

Adventure Tours: If you're looking for a thrilling experience, think about going on an adventure trip that involves off-roading, rock climbing, or canyoning. These trips provide a unique approach to viewing the island's challenging landscape and are tailored for thrill-seekers. Look into adventure vacations offered by organizations such as Xtravel (www.xtravel.es) and Climbo (www.climbo.rocks).From island hopping and boat tours to guided cultural, wildlife, and adventure tours, Gran Canaria offers a wide range of day trips and excursions to suit every interest. These encounters guarantee a fascinating and enlightening stay by enabling you to completely appreciate the varied beauty and rich culture of Gran Canaria and its adjacent islands.

PRACTICAL INFORMATION

Useful Advice for Visitors to Gran Canaria Understanding the practical elements of your vacation to Gran Canaria can help you have a more pleasurable and seamless stay. This comprehensive book provides all the necessary practical information on the language, money, banking, electricity, time zone, and customs and etiquette of the area.

Words Official tongue:

Gran Canaria is a part of Spain, hence Spanish is the official language of the island. Canarian Spanish is the name given to the regional dialect, which differs somewhat from mainland Spanish in vocabulary and accent. For example, the final sound in nouns is often missing or aspirated.

Languages Other Than English: The majority of people in tourist regions speak English, particularly in restaurants, stores, and hotels. Because so many people travel from Europe, many residents who work in the tourist industry are also fluent in German and other European languages.

Practical Expressions: Acquiring a few fundamental Spanish phrases may be quite beneficial and well-received by the natives. Here are a few typical ones: Hi there: HelloRegards and thanks: Thank you would you please: PleasePardon me: Perdón¿Dónde está?: Where is...?What is the price? ¿Cuánto cuesta?

Money and Banking Currency

The Euro (€) is the currency in use in Gran Canaria. Coins are available in 1, 2, 5, 10, 20, and 50 cent values in addition to €1 and €2, while banknotes are available in the following denominations: €5, €10, €20, €50, €100, €200, and €500.Financial Services: Banks abound, particularly in bigger cities and popular tourist destinations. Usually, they are open from 8:30 AM to 2:00 PM, **Monday through Friday.** Certain locations could open on Saturday mornings.

ATMs: ATMs are often located and may be found at banks, retail establishments, and tourist destinations. The majority of **ATMs accept major debit and credit cards,** such as MasterCard and Visa. It's a good idea to verify in advance since there can be costs associated with foreign withdrawals from your home bank.

Currency Exchange: At airports, hotels, and specific exchange offices, currency exchange services are offered. To receive the greatest bargain, it is important to compare rates and fees. Rates at exchange offices are usually more favorable than those at hotels or airports.

Interaction Internet connectivity Wi-Fi

Public spaces like airports and shopping centers often provide free Wi-Fi, as do cafés, restaurants, and hotels. Make sure you request the password if it isn't readily apparent. Internet cafes: These establishments charge a fee for computer access for anyone without access to their equipment. Although they are not as widespread as they once were, they may still be found in certain places.

Mobile Internet: You might think about getting a local SIM card with a data package if you need a continuous internet connection. Prepaid SIM cards are available from well-known carriers like Movistar, Vodafone, and Orange, which you can top up as required.

Coverage of Mobile Networks: 4G/LTE services are available across Gran Canaria, with typically good mobile network coverage. Vodafone, Orange, Yoigo, and Movistar are a few of the major mobile providers.

SIM Cards: Mobile phone shops, convenience stores, and supermarkets carry local SIM cards. You may have to provide your ID or passport to buy a SIM card. For travelers, prepaid SIM cards are a cost-effective option since they provide reasonable prices for data, texts, and calls.

Roaming: According to EU legislation, you may use a European SIM card in Gran Canaria without paying extra roaming fees. However, for precise information and any possible limitations, speak with your provider.

Plugs and electricity Voltage and Frequency

50Hz is the standard frequency and 230V is the standard voltage in Gran Canaria.

Types of Plugs: Type C (two round pins) and Type F (two round pins with two earth clips on the side) are the two types of plugs and sockets. You'll need an appropriate adaptor if the plugs on your gadgets are different.

Converters and Adapters: Travel adapters are generally accessible and may be bought at electronics shops, some supermarkets, and airports. You may also need a voltage converter if the voltage of your gadget is incompatible with the local voltage.

Zone of Time Standard Time: Western European Time (WET), often known as Greenwich Mean Time (GMT), is used in Gran Canaria.

Daylight Saving Time: Gran Canaria observes Western European Summer Time **(WEST), or GMT+1,** from the last Sunday in March to the last Sunday in October.

Regional Traditions and ProtocolsSalutations: In Spanish culture, a kind salutation is highly valued. In official contexts, people shake hands, but friends and relatives often kiss each other on the cheeks as they meet one another.Courtesy and politeness are highly regarded. It is customary to use **"please"** (favor) and **"thank you"** (gracias). It is customary to say "Buenos días" (good morning) or **"buenas tardes"** (good afternoon) to people as you enter stores or restaurants.

Dining Protocol: It is usual to wait to begin eating while dining out until everyone has been served. Tipping is customary but not required; at restaurants, it's typical to round up the bill or leave between 5 and 10%.

Dress Code: Although casual wear is appropriate in most places, it is appropriate to wear modest clothing when visiting places of worship. Beachwear is not suitable in town or public areas; it is only appropriate at the beach or pool.

Siesta: In certain areas of Gran Canaria, especially in the smaller towns, the siesta custom is still followed. Stores and companies may shut in the afternoon for a few hours, often from 2:00 PM to 5:00 PM, and then reopen in the evening.

Public Behavior: It is customary to discourage boisterous and disruptive conduct. Public expressions of love are permitted as long as they follow regional customs.

Environmental Respect: The preservation of the environment is highly valued in Gran Canaria. Respect the environment by avoiding littering, following local regulations for the protection of animals, and keeping on trails that are designated in natural parks.Photography: Before taking a picture of someone, always get their consent, particularly in remote locations or during important occasions. Be mindful of signage that prohibits taking pictures, especially in places of worship and museums.

Emergency Numbers: Dial 112 to get police, fire, or ambulance help right away in an emergency. Pharmacies and health clinics are open around the clock for non-urgent medical needs.

You may guarantee a more pleasant and courteous experience by being aware of and mindful of these practical elements of living in Gran Canaria. With this understanding, **you will be able to enjoy the island's culture, traverse it with ease, and get the most out of your trip.**

BUSINESS AND CONFERENCES

Known for its breathtaking scenery and dynamic culture, Gran Canaria is a great place for **conferences and business travel.** The **island is a great place for business meetings**, conferences, and professional get-togethers since it has modern conference facilities, hotels that cater to business travelers, and plenty of networking possibilities. This comprehensive guide will assist you in organizing your business trip to Gran Canaria.

Conference Rooms Gran Canaria

Facilities: INFECAR has several adaptable facilities, such as a 1,200-seat main auditorium, several smaller conference rooms, and large exhibition halls.

Services: The center offers a wide range of services, including help with event planning, technical support, and catering.

Contact information: 35005 Las Palmas de Gran Canaria, Spain; Calle León y Castillo, 230. Tel: (34 928465400). Email address: info@infecar.es. INFECAR's website 2.

Auditorio Alfredo Kraus: This recognizable auditorium is a spectacular location for conferences and cultural events. It is situated on Las Canteras Beach in Las Palmas.

Facilities: The auditorium comprises a main hall with a seating capacity of 2,000, different smaller conference rooms, and a huge display space.
Services: It provides expert event planning, catering, and cutting-edge audiovisual equipment. Av. Príncipe de Asturias, s/n, 35010 Las Palmas de Gran Canaria, Spain is the address to contact. Telephone: (34 9284 7707). Contact info@auditoriokraus.es via email. Alfredo Kraus Auditorio website.

ExpoMeloneras: This contemporary convention facility is perfect for sizable gatherings and exhibits and is situated in the resort community of Meloneras, close to Maspalomas.

Facilities: ExpoMeloneras has many breakout rooms, a sizable conference hall that can accommodate up to 5,000 people and a considerable amount of display space. Services: Full-service event management is provided, including technical assistance, catering, and audiovisual support. Contact information: 1 Calle Mar Mediterráneo, Meloneras, 35100, Spain. Contact: (34 928128 000).

Contact info@expomeloneras.com via email. The ExpoMeloneras website.

Business - Friendly Hotel

Hotels That Are Business-Friendly Gran Canaria has a range of hotels that are ideal for business visitors, offering first-rate lodging and amenities.

Hotel Santa Catalina, a Royal Hideaway Hotel: This opulent Las Palmas hotel blends contemporary conveniences with a historic charm.

Facilities: The hotel has a business center, many conference rooms, and fast internet. Gourmet restaurants, a fitness facility, and a spa are all included.

Services: Concierge, transportation arrangements, and event preparation are examples of business services. Calle León y Castillo, 227, 35005 Las Palmas de Gran Canaria, Spain is the address to contact. Telephone: (928) 243-040. Santacatalina@royalhideaway.com is her email. Santa Catalina Hotel website

Seaside Palm Beach Hotel: This five-star establishment, which is close to Maspalomas, gives business visitors a chic environment. Amenities include meeting spaces, a business center, and high-speed internet access. It also has pools, great restaurants, and a wellness center.
Services: Transportation, catering, and event planning are examples of professional services.

Contact information: Avenida del Oasis, s/n, Maspalomas, Spain, 35100. Call: (34 9287-721) 032. Contact info@hotel-palm-beach.com via email.

Website: Palm Beach by the Sea.

Hotel Reina Isabel & Spa: This Las Palmas hotel is well situated and provides easy access to both business and recreational facilities. Facilities: The hotel offers free Wi-Fi, a business center, and many conference spaces. A restaurant on the beach, a spa, and a rooftop pool are available to visitors.

Services: Transportation arrangements, meeting preparation, and secretarial help are examples of business services. Alfredo L. Jones, 40, 35008 Las Palmas de Gran Canaria, Spain is the address to contact. Telephone: (928)

260-100. Contact info@hotelreinaisabel.com via email. Hotel Reina Isabel's website.

Networking opportunities

Opportunities for Networking Business executives may take advantage of a range of networking opportunities in Gran Canaria. Participating in regional and global business communities may strengthen your network and lead to new opportunities for cooperation.

Business groups and Chambers of Commerce: A great approach to network with other professionals is to become a member of your local chamber of commerce and business groups. Regular events, seminars, and networking meetings are arranged by the Cámara de Comercio de Gran Canaria, also known as the Gran Canaria Chamber of Commerce.Calle León y Castillo, 24 35003 Las Palmas de Gran Canaria, Spain is the address to contact. Telephone: (928) 390-390. Contact info@camaragrancanaria.org via email. Cámara de Comercio is the website.

Professional Events and Trade exhibits: Throughout the year, Gran Canaria is home to a large number of professional events and trade exhibits. You may network with business partners, customers, and industry experts by taking part in these events. For information on forthcoming conferences and trade shows, check the event calendars of locations like ExpoMeloneras and INFECAR.

Co-Working Spaces: These places are excellent for networking with other professionals, independent contractors, and business owners. They facilitate teamwork and often arrange lectures, workshops, and networking activities. Two well-known co-working spaces in Gran Canaria are Soppa de Azul (www.soppadeazul.com) and The House (www.thehousecw.com).

Business Networking organizations: Several clubs and networking organizations gather regularly to discuss business prospects, share ideas, and cultivate professional connections. Organizations that provide formal networking opportunities include the Rotary Club and BNI (Business Network International) Gran Canaria.

Online Resources and Social Media: Make use of online resources such as LinkedIn to establish connections with nearby business people and remain updated on networking gatherings and business prospects in Gran Canaria. To interact with the community, join **forums and business groups in your area.**

Gran Canaria is a great location for conferences and business travel, with first-rate amenities, lodging that is conducive to business, and plenty of networking opportunities. The facilities and services offered by Gran Canaria can suit all of your demands, **whether you're organizing a small business gathering or a major international conference.** You can guarantee a fruitful and profitable business vacation while also taking in Gran Canaria's stunning surroundings and vibrant culture by making the most of the island's resources.

SPECIAL INTEREST TRAVEL

Gran Canaria is a place that offers more than simply sun and beach. It provides a wide range of activities for travelers with specific interests, from adventure travel like whitewater rafting, canyoning, caving, and exploration to wine tours and wellness retreats. **This comprehensive guide will assist you in discovering these distinctive features of the island.**

Wine Tours and Vineyard Visits

Wine Tours and Visits to VineyardsGran Canaria has a growing wine culture, owing in part to its distinct and tasty wines produced by its volcanic soil and unusual environment. For any wine connoisseur, wine excursions and vineyard visits are essential.

Bodegas Las Tirajanas: This island's centrally located winery provides a thorough wine experience. Visitors may take a tour of the vineyards, taste a selection of wines, and learn about the wine-making process.

Highlights of the program include a guided vineyard tour, a sample of the wine, and an optional lunch.Contact information: San Bartolomé de Tirajana, Gran Canaria, Spain; Calle La Longuera, 1, 35280. (34 9228 798 405) phone. Contact info@bodegastirajanas.com via email. Bodegas Las Tirajanas' website.

Bodega Los Berrazales: This Agaete Valley winery, maintained by a family, is well-known for both its beautiful setting and its excellent wines. A tour of the fruit orchards, coffee farms, and vineyards is available to visitors.Highlights of the trip include a visit to a vineyard and plantation, a sample of local vegetables and wine, and coffee.Lugar Diseminado Valle de Agaete, 9, 35480 Agaete, Gran Canaria, Spain is the address to contact. **Tel: (34 928554139).** Bodega Los Berrazales website; email: info@bodegalosberrazales.com.

Bodega Hoyos de Bandama: This winery, which is close to the Bandama Caldera, is known for its great wines and breathtaking scenery. The volcanic soil of the caldera imparts a distinct taste character to the wines.Highlights of the excursion include wine tasting, a guided vineyard tour, a visit to the Bandama Caldera, and a pairing of local cheeses. Los Hoyos, 154, 35017 Las Palmas, Gran Canaria, Spain is the address to contact. Caller number: +34 928 351-331. Contact info@bodegahoyosdebandama.com via email. Bodega Hoyos de Bandama's website.

Wellness and Spa Retreats

Spa and Wellness GetawaysGran Canaria is the ideal location for anyone looking to unwind and revitalize themselves. Numerous top-notch health and spa resorts providing a variety of therapies and treatments may be found on the island.

Gloria Palace San Agustín Thalasso & Hotel: This establishment has one of the biggest thalassotherapy facilities in Europe, providing treatments based on saltwater that are intended to enhance health and wellbeing.Facilities include a Turkish bath, a thalassotherapy pool, several saunas, relaxation areas, and an extensive treatment menu.
Get in touch: Calle Las Margaritas, s/n, Gran Canaria, Spain, 35100 San Agustín. Tel: (334) 928-128-505. Contact: sanagustin@gloriapalaceth.com via email. Gloria Palace San Agustín website

Bohemia Suites & Spa: This adult-only resort in Playa del Inglés provides opulent spa treatments along with

breathtaking views of the ocean.Facilities include a Turkish bath, sauna, rooftop wellness center, and individualized treatments.Avenida Estados Unidos, 28, 35100 Playa del Inglés, Gran Canaria, Spain is the address to contact. Tel: (34 9285-6340).
Email address: info@grancanaria.bohemia.com. Bohemia Suites & Spa website.

Lopesan Costa Meloneras Resort, Spa & Casino: This Meloneras resort has an opulent spa offering a variety of treatments as well as a lovely garden setting.Facilities include massage rooms, thermal baths, a hydrotherapy circuit, and beauty services.Mar Mediterráneo, 1, 35100 Meloneras, Gran Canaria, Spain is the address to reach. Telephone: (928) 128 100. Email address: lopesan.com/costameloneras. Lopesan Costa Meloneras' website.

Adventure Tourism

Gran Canaria has a variety of adventure tourism activities to suit the interests of outdoor enthusiasts and adrenaline seekers. Every explorer may find something to enjoy on the island, from alpine activities to aquatic sports.

Canoeing and Rafting

Gran Canaria's varied topography offers exceptional possibilities for canyoning, an adventure activity that entails traversing through gorges utilizing a variety of tactics including walking, climbing, and swimming. Gran Canaria may not be the first spot that springs to mind when thinking about rafting.

Canyoning with Climbo: Climbo provides guided trips for canyoning that take you through some of the island's most breathtaking natural settings.Experience: Make your way through deep pools, natural slides, and waterfalls. Appropriate for both novice and seasoned explorers.Phone number to reach: +34 686 682 370. Website: Climbo. Email: info@climbo.rocks.

Canyoning with Mojo Picon Aventura: Located all around Gran Canaria, Mojo Picon Aventura offers thrilling canyoning excursions. Experience: All required equipment is given, and knowledgeable guides guarantee a fun and safe expedition.Phone number to reach: **+34 637 815 051.** contact@mojopiconaventura.com via email. Mojo Picon Aventura's website

Exploration and Caving: Because of its volcanic past, Gran Canaria has an amazing system of caverns and subterranean passageways that are ideal for exploring.

The Painted Cave, or Cueva Pintada: This archaeological site, which is situated in Gáldar, provides an intriguing look into the pre-Hispanic history of the island. It offers an interesting and instructive investigation even if it isn't a typical caving experience.

Experience: Guided tours of the museum's exhibits and the painted walls of the cave. Calle Audiencia, 2, 35460 Gáldar, Gran Canaria, Spain is the address to reach. Phone: +34 895 746 928. Contact cuevapintada@grancanaria.com via email. The Cueva Pintada website

Caving with Canarias Caveland

Spelunking trips into some of the island's natural caverns are conducted by Caveland Canarias, for those looking for a more daring caving experience.

Experience: With knowledgeable guides, explore subterranean passageways, rooms, and formations. Phone number to reach: **+34 609 514 833.** Contact info@cavelandcanarias.com via email. Caveland Canarias' website. In summary, Canaria is a great place for special interest tourism because of its varied scenery and rich cultural legacy.

The island has plenty to offer everyone, whether they are wine enthusiasts, hoping to unwind at a spa resort, or adventure seekers searching for their next big thrill. **Making sure that your trip to Gran Canaria is both gratifying and unforgettable,** the activities described in this book provide a unique and fascinating approach to discovering the numerous elements of the island.

GRAN CANARIA ON A BUDGET

Gran Canaria is a stunning location that is worth visiting even on a limited budget. There are many methods to make the most of your trip without going over budget, from free and inexpensive activities to reasonably priced restaurants and lodging options. This comprehensive guide will assist you in organizing an affordable vacation to this beautiful island.

Free and Low-Cost Attractions

Gran Canaria has an abundance of free or inexpensive natural beauty, cultural events, and historical places. Here are a few highly suggested items.

Las Canteras Beach: Known as one of Gran Canaria's most popular beaches, this spot is ideal for swimming, snorkeling, and tanning. You may walk along the lengthy promenade, people-watch, or have a picnic there.

Vegueta Old Town: Take a tour of Las Palmas, Vegueta's historic quarter, where you can take in the colorful plazas, cobblestone streets, and colonial buildings. Important locations include the Casa de Colón, a relatively reasonably priced museum devoted to Christopher Columbus's expeditions, and the Santa Ana Cathedral.

Pico de las Nieves: The island's highest peak, Pico de las Nieves, offers stunning vistas. The overlook provides expansive views of the island. It's a fantastic location for shooting pictures and admiring the island's scenic charm.

Roque Nublo: Another remarkable natural feature, Roque Nublo is a well-known sight in Gran Canaria. It's affordable to hike to Roque Nublo, which offers breathtaking views of the untamed terrain of the island.

Jardín Botánico Viera y Clavijo: A wide range of Canary Island native plant species may be found in this large botanical garden. It's a great place for a stroll and learning about the local flora.

Maspalomas Dunes: This exceptional natural reserve allows you to stroll over enormous, desert-like dunes. It is a cheap day out at the next beach.

Mercado de Vegueta: Take a peek at the lively Vegueta Market in Las Palmas to get a taste of the local way of life, try some fresh vegetables, and maybe score some reasonably priced mementos. It costs nothing to browse the market, and you may buy refreshments at affordable pricing.

Museo Canario: Using items from the native Guanche people, this museum in Las Palmas provides insights into the pre-Hispanic history of the island. The relatively affordable admission price makes it an affordable cultural experience.

Affordable Eateries

There are several affordable eating alternatives available in Gran Canaria. These reasonably priced restaurants provide mouthwatering regional cuisine without breaking the bank.

Churrería Cafetería Mercado de Vegueta: This restaurant, which is part of the Vegueta Market, is well-known for its reasonably priced and delicious coffee and churros. It's a terrific spot for an inexpensive breakfast or snack.

Tasca El Canalla: A well-liked location in Las Palmas, Tasca El Canalla serves affordable Spanish cuisine in addition to a wide selection of tapas. The wonderful cuisine and vibrant environment make it an excellent option for a budget-friendly supper.

La Vegueta de Colón: A variety of Canarian and Spanish cuisine is served at this little Vegueta restaurant. Travelers on a tight budget might consider this choice since the menu is fairly priced and the quantities are substantial.

Clandestino: Located in Las Palmas, this restaurant serves a variety of delectable, reasonably priced meals with an emphasis on locally sourced, fresh ingredients. They provide exceptional value for money with their set meals and daily specials.

El Rincon de Omar: This Puerto Rican eatery is well-known for its good and reasonably priced pasta, pizza, and other Italian fare. Both residents and visitors searching for an affordable eating choice love it.

Mercado del Puerto: Several food vendors at this Las Palmas market provide a range of reasonably priced meals, including seafood and foreign cuisine. You may try a variety of foods there without going over budget.

Budget-Friendly Accommodation

Affordable Place to Stay Gran Canaria offers a variety of inexpensive lodging alternatives, from hostels to reasonably priced hotels and vacation homes. The following suggestions are provided.

Avocado Surf Hostel: This Las Palmas hostel has a range of lodging choices, including private rooms and dorm beds. For those on a tight budget who want to mingle and socialize, it's a fantastic option.

HiTide House: Located near Las Canteras Beach, HiTide House is yet another fantastic hostel in Las Palmas. It's an affordable alternative with wonderful facilities, including a rooftop patio, community kitchen, and both private and dorm rooms.

Aparthotel Riosol: This reasonably priced aparthotel in Puerto Rico provides self-catering apartments with kitchenettes to help you cut down on eating out. The resort has a swimming pool.

Hotel Verol: Located in Las Palmas, this affordable hotel provides cozy accommodations at fair rates. Las Canteras Beach and a variety of eateries and other establishments are nearby.

Hostal Alcaravaneras: This affordable hostel in Las Palmas is close to Alcaravaneras Beach and has simple yet tidy accommodations. It's a fantastic choice for tourists searching for reasonably priced lodging in a convenient area.

Airbnb and Vacation properties: Airbnb and other such sites provide a large number of reasonably priced vacation properties on Gran Canaria. For families or groups in particular, renting an apartment or home might be a financially advantageous choice.

Canaria on a Budget

Gran Canaria has several campgrounds and glamping choices for outdoor enthusiasts. For those who like the outdoors, Camping El Pinillo, which is close to Tamadaba

Natural Park, is an inexpensive choice. Advice for Low-Cost Vacationers

Plan: You may get better discounts if you reserve your travel and lodging in advance. Online, look for deals and discounts.

Take Public Transportation: The public transportation system in Gran Canaria is economical and effective. When traveling the island, buses are a wonderful alternative to expensive taxis or auto rentals.

Prepare Your Meals: If your lodging has a kitchen, think about preparing some of your meals. Reasonably priced fresh vegetables are available at local markets.

Affordable Walking Tours: Discover the history and culture of the island without paying for guided tours by taking advantage of affordable walking tours offered in Las Palmas and other locations.

Go Off-Season: You can get great deals on flights and lodging by going to Gran Canaria off-season, and you'll also be able to escape the crowds.

You may have an unforgettable vacation to Gran Canaria without breaking the bank if you implement these suggestions and take advantage of the reasonably priced choices that are available. Your experience shouldn't be sacrificed, whether you're seeing breathtaking beaches, **enjoying regional food, or lodging at an affordable price.**

NEW UPDATES AND EXPECTATIONS IN GRAN CANARIA FOR 2024

Gran Canaria, one of the most popular travel destinations in the Canary Islands, is always changing to improve the experiences it offers tourists. Several intriguing changes and additions are **anticipated for 2024, which will increase the island's allure.** This is a comprehensive look at what Gran Canaria has in store for visitors in 2024, including everything from new events and attractions to infrastructure upgrades and environmental programs.

New Developments and Attraction

Maspalomas Theme Park expansion: This well-liked theme park has grown significantly, adding new rides and attractions for both thrill-seekers and families. The park's attraction has been increased and it is now a must-visit **location in 2024** thanks to the addition of many new roller coasters, water rides, and themed zones.

Gran Canaria Aquarium opens: Visitors can now explore the marine biodiversity of the Canary Islands and beyond at this cutting-edge aquarium located in Las Palmas. Numerous displays are available at the **Gran Canaria** Aquarium, such as an expansive ocean tank including sharks and rays, interactive touch pools, and teaching initiatives centered on marine conservation.

Improved Hiking paths: Better signs, rest spaces, and safety precautions have been added to a number of the breathtaking hiking paths that make Gran Canaria renowned. The well-liked paths to Roque Nublo and Pico de las Nieves are noteworthy additions that enhance accessibility and enjoyment for hikers of all skill levels on these trails.

New Cultural facilities: Several brand-new cultural facilities highlighting Gran Canaria's rich history are scheduled to debut in 2024. Exhibitions, seminars, and performances showcasing Canarian history, art, and customs will take place at these centers.

The enlargement of Casa de Colón, which now has a new wing devoted to the native Guanche culture, is one noteworthy feature.

Initiatives for Sustainability

Green Tourism Initiatives: In 2024, Gran Canaria will intensify its efforts to promote eco-friendly travel. The island has launched several green tourism initiatives, including programs that encourage visitors to engage in environmental conservation efforts, eco-friendly lodging alternatives, and sustainable transportation options.

Renewable Energy Projects: Throughout Gran Canaria, substantial sums of money have been invested in renewable energy projects. To lessen the island's carbon impact and encourage the use of renewable energy, new wind and solar farms are being built. Additionally, more green energy-powered public transportation options and charging facilities for electric vehicles will be visible to visitors.

Plastic Reduction drive: Gran Canaria has initiated a significant drive to cut down on single-use plastics. This project aims to reduce plastic waste by educating visitors, encouraging local companies to embrace sustainable practices, and outlawing plastic straws and bags in favor of biodegradable alternatives.

Infrastructure Upgrades

Improved Public Transportation: New, environmentally friendly buses and redesigned routes to better accommodate both residents and visitors have been added to Gran Canaria's public transportation system. Getting around will be more practical and effective with the installation of fast lines linking the island's capital, Las Palmas, with popular tourist destinations.

Airport Improvements: To enhance the traveler experience, **Gran Canaria Airport (LPA)** has undergone significant modifications. Increased facilities including lounges, dining choices, and retail stores are among the improvements, along with larger terminals and more security checks. The goal of these upgrades is to make travel easier and provide guests with a more relaxing experience.

Road Improvements: To enhance safety and traffic flow, a number of the island's main thoroughfares have been modernized. Significant improvements have been made to the GC-1 roadway, which links Las Palmas to the southern tourist destinations. These improvements include the addition of lanes and improved signage. Driving around the island will be safer and more effective with these upgrades.

Occasions and Celebrations

Gran Canaria Carnival: One of the island's most colorful yearly celebrations, the Gran Canaria Carnival, is expected to become even larger and better in 2024. This year's carnival offers additional entertainment and chances to immerse oneself in Canarian culture with an extended schedule of parades, concerts, and cultural events.

International Music Festival: In 2024, Gran Canaria will host its first-ever international music festival, which is expected to draw world-class musicians. From classical to modern music, a wide range of musical styles will be performed at this event, which will take place in breathtaking outdoor spaces all across the island.

Gastronomy Weeks: In 2024, several gastronomy weeks honoring the island's culinary legacy will take place on Gran Canaria. Special menus at neighborhood eateries, cooking classes, and food markets featuring Canarian produce and regional cuisine will all be featured at these events.

Provision and Warmth

New Boutique Hotels: Several distinctive and opulent boutique hotels with an emphasis on regional culture and sustainability are popping up across Gran Canaria. These lodging establishments provide individualized services, amenities supplied locally, and engaging experiences that let visitors connect with the island's history.

Eco-Friendly Resorts: New eco-friendly resorts are being built in response to the rising demand for environmentally responsible vacation choices. While providing opulent luxuries, these resorts reduce their environmental effect by using eco-friendly construction materials, renewable energy sources, and water conservation techniques.

Renovated All-Inclusive Resorts: To improve their services, already-existing all-inclusive resorts are being renovated. Upgrades to the facilities, a wider variety of food choices, and new programs like adventure excursions and health centers are all examples of improvements. The purpose of these improvements is to provide visitors with a better value and a more engaging experience.

Innovation and Technology

Smart Tourism: To improve tourist experiences, Gran Canaria is using smart tourism technologies. Real-time information about attractions, events, and services is being made available via the introduction of new applications and digital platforms. Travelers will find it easier to traverse the island and get tailored suggestions with the aid of these tools.

Free Wi-Fi Zones: Gran Canaria is growing its network of free Wi-Fi zones to make sure that tourists remain connected. These zones facilitate information access and family communication for tourists by being present at prominent tourist destinations, public transit hubs, and significant tourist sites.

Virtual Tours and Augmented Reality: Major Gran Canaria attractions are developing cutting-edge virtual tours and augmented reality experiences. With the use of these technologies, tourists may discover historical landmarks and breathtaking natural formations in fresh and captivating ways that provide opportunities for participatory learning and deeper insights.

Canaria's new attractions, upgraded infrastructure, and creative tourist initiatives aim to make the island even more fascinating and sustainable in 2024. These changes and advancements guarantee that your vacation will be fun, memorable, and environmentally friendly—whether you're a first-time visitor or a returnee. Organize your trip to take advantage of all this beautiful island has to offer while **keeping up with the most recent developments and products.**

LOCAL INSIGHTS

The lively island of Gran Canaria is home to a diverse range of customs, civilizations, and individual tales. It is crucial to hear from the people who live there in order to comprehend the spirit of this stunning location. In this area, we present firsthand accounts of the island's most beloved events and dive into local perspectives via interviews with locals.

Interviews with Gran Canaria Residents

These stories provide an insight into the customs, festivals, and sense of camaraderie that characterize Gran Canaria. Conversations with Citizens of Gran Canaria Interview with Local Historian María Fernández

What is your favorite thing about residing in Gran Canaria?
María: I like this place's mix of environments and civilizations. Gran Canaria provides a range of landscapes, from the golden sands of Maspalomas in the south to the verdant forests in the north. There is a strong feeling of community and a profound connection to history and

customs. Festivals are how we honor our ancestry, and there's always a tale to tell.

Could you tell us about a historical location that has particular meaning for you?
María: Gáldar's Painted Cave is very noteworthy. It provides a glimpse of the Guanches', the native Canarian people, way of life. The distinctive cave drawings provide details about their customs and manner of life. It serves as a reminder of our lengthy and rich past.

Q&A with Local Chef Carlos Rodríguez: What is your favorite meal to make in the Canary Islands?

Carlos: I like cooking. This traditional meal consists of potatoes, chickpeas, shredded meat, and spices. It's a fantastic illustration of how Canarian cooking combines many influences.
It's a food that unites people, and every family has their twist on it.

Q: Where do you get your ingredients from?

Carlos: I make utilizing local products a priority. Gran Canaria has excellent markets with a wide variety of fresh produce, fish, and fruits. When ingredients are purchased locally, the tastes are more intense. Supporting regional fishers and farmers is crucial for sustainability and our community.

Interview with Festival Organizer Elena Martín.

What distinguishes the Gran Canaria Carnival from others?

Elena: The Gran Canaria Carnival is an amazing fusion of culture, music, and color. The fact that the whole town participates makes it one of the liveliest events on the island. Everyone gathers to celebrate life and creativity, from the spectacular procession to the street celebrations. The outfits are amazing, particularly during the Drag Queen Gala.

How is the local community involved in the event organized?

Elena: From planning to implementation, the community is involved from the first. Contributions to the floats, costumes, and performances come from local cultural organizations, schools, and artists. Everyone takes satisfaction in exhibiting their ingenuity and cultural heritage, and it's a team effort.

Individual Narratives of Gran Canaria Festivals José's Fiesta de San Juan ExperienceA Las Palmas native for his whole life, José Pérez talks about his memories of the Fiesta de San Juan, a beach party, fireworks, and bonfire festival that ushers in summer.

José: "One of my favorite celebrations is the Fiesta de San Juan. The whole city comes to life on this particular night. On Las Canteras Beach, people congregate, and as the sun sets, bonfires are lit.

Watching the flames dance beneath the night sky has a certain enchantment. We think that leaping over the campfire clears our spirits and brings luck.

My family and I cook traditional Canarian foods like mojo sauce and papas for our annual picnic. Around the fire, we sing, dance, and tell tales. The midnight fireworks show is the highlight. The ocean reflects many hues, creating a breathtaking image. This is a night of happiness, humor, and camaraderie.

Romería de Santiago de Gáldar: Ana's StoryGáldar native Ana García, a schoolteacher, relates her recollections of the town's customary pilgrimage commemorating its patron saint, the Romería de Santiago de Gáldar. Ana: "**We see great spiritual and cultural significance in the Romería de Santiago**. Each year, we don traditional Canarian clothing and go through Gáldar's neighborhoods, bringing bread, fruit, and vegetable offerings to the Santiago de los Caballeros church. As a youngster, I recall taking part in the romería with my grandparents. It was a chance to express gratitude and strengthen our ties to our past. Folk bands with guitars and temples are performing all over the streets. Traditional Canarian dances such as the "**isa" and "folía"** are also performed.

We all congregate in the town plaza for a community feast after the parade. It's a day to celebrate our origins, give thanks, and reflect. It's an honor to pass these traditions on to the next generation since there is a strong feeling of community and heritage." **Miguel's** Narrative from the Flor Fiesta del Almendro Tejeda farmer Miguel Sánchez talks about his experience at the Fiesta del Almendro en Flor, a celebration honoring the almond blooms that signal the start of spring. Miguel: "**Nature** and agriculture are beautifully celebrated at the Fiesta del Almendro en Flor. The almond trees in Tejeda bloom in February, blanketing the surrounding area with dainty pink and white blossoms.

Visitors from all around the island come to see this breathtaking sight.

This holiday is very meaningful to me since I am a farmer. It's a moment to honor the toil and commitment required to cultivate the land. Traditional crafts, dances, and music are all included during the event. We put up booths where we sold pastries, almond milk, and marzipan, among other almond-based goods. The **'almond picking contest,'** in which players vie to collect almonds as quickly as possible, is one of my favorite aspects.

It's a vibrant and enjoyable event that unites the neighborhood. The Fiesta del Almendro en Flor serves as a wonderful reminder of the abundance and natural beauty of our island, as well as the need to protect our agricultural legacy.

Canaria's rich cultural tapestry may be seen from a different angle thanks to the local perspectives and firsthand accounts of the island's events. We learn more about the customs, sense of community, and way of life that make Gran Canaria such a unique location via the words of its people. These experiences showcase the island's distinct character and the pride its inhabitants have in their history, whether it's via the colorful festivities of the Gran Canaria Carnival, **the spiritual journey of the Romería de Santiago, or the natural beauty of the Fiesta del Almendro en Flor.**

CONCLUSION

As you approach the conclusion of our all-inclusive Gran Canaria travel guide, take a moment to consider the amazing adventures this magical island has in store for you. Gran Canaria is more than simply a travel destination; it's a veritable gold mine of breathtaking scenery, fascinating local culture, and life-changing experiences. Let's explore more about what makes Gran Canaria the ideal location for your next vacation.

Final Thoughts on Gran Canaria

Gran Canaria is home to a breathtaking variety of scenery, ranging from lush mountains and charming towns to sun-kissed beaches and towering sand dunes. Explore the island's hidden treasures and learn about its fascinating history; every corner provides a different and engaging experience.

Basking in the Sand and Sunlight: A day spent relaxing on Gran Canaria's immaculate beaches is a must-do activity for every visitor. There are many places to take advantage of the warm weather on the island, whether you like the busy beaches of Playa del Inglés or the quiet coves of Puerto de Mogán.

Advice: If you want a really unique beach experience, think about reserving a room at one of Gran Canaria's beachfront resorts, where you can have direct access to the sand and wake up to the sound of the waves.

Investigating Historical Places and Cultural Assets:
Numerous historic structures and cultural landmarks in Gran Canaria are testament to the island's rich past. There are several intriguing sites to discover, such as the historic cave homes of Artenara and the colonial architecture of Vegueta.

Price: Generally speaking, admission costs to museums and historic sites vary from €5 to €15 per person, with student, elder, and child reductions available.

Snacking on Gourmet Treats: The rich tapestry of tastes and influences that makes up Gran Canaria's culinary culture highlights the island's rich cultural legacy. There are many delectable selections to suit your appetite, whether you're in the mood for foreign cuisine, fresh seafood, or traditional Canarian cuisine.

Cost: While street food and informal dining establishments provide more affordable alternatives beginning at €5, mid-range restaurants usually charge between €15 and €30 per person for their meals.

Exploring the Great Outdoors for Adventure:
Gran Canaria is an adventurer's paradise just waiting to be discovered. In the midst of the island's breathtaking natural beauty, there are plenty of heart-pounding activities to do, including hiking, mountain biking, surfing, and scuba diving.

Cost: Depending on the supplier and the length of the event, prices for outdoor activities vary. For equipment rentals and guided trips, budget between €20 and €100.

Unwinding in Elegance and Coziness:
Nothing compares to relaxing in the lap of luxury at one of Gran Canaria's posh resorts or spa retreats after a day of exploration and excitement. Indulge in a fine dining experience, pamper yourself with a massage, or just unwind by the pool and take in the stunning scenery.

Cost: Depending on the business and degree of quality, costs for opulent lodging and spa services vary. A luxurious hotel room may set you back up to €100 per night, and a spa treatment could set you back at least €50.

Getting In Touch with Local Communities and Cultures: Connecting with the lively local people and culture of Gran Canaria is one of the most fulfilling vacation experiences. The friendliness and kindness of the locals are just as enticing as the breathtaking scenery, whether you're attending a traditional fiesta, perusing the local market, or starting up a discussion with a local acquaintance.

Price: While some cultural events and community activities may charge an entry fee or modest payment, many are free to attend. For information on forthcoming events and activities, see your local listings.

Organizing Your Upcoming Journey

The experiences you have created on **Gran Canaria will last a lifetime,** so keep that in mind when you say goodbye and start making plans for your next journey. The world is yours to explore, whether your dreams are of going back to uncover more of Gran Canaria's hidden gems or of traveling to a new place.

To get the most out of your next journey, think about scheduling a personalized travel package or enrolling in a guided tour. You may design an itinerary that suits your interests and tastes with the assistance of skilled planners and informed guides.

Gran Canaria is a place that really has it all: amazing natural beauty, engrossing history and culture, delectable food, and many options for leisure and adventure. This incredible island has everything and more to offer those seeking adventure, excitement, or quiet and relaxation.

So, **why do you hesitate?**

Gran Canaria awaits your next trip. Prepare for the voyage of a lifetime by packing your luggage, focusing on the far distance, and starting out on the right path. **Are you prepared to answer the call from Gran Canaria?**

FREQUENTLY ASKED QUESTIONS

You can have several inquiries about Gran Canaria, its attractions, transportation, and other topics as you organize your vacation. Here are some often-asked questions and their thorough answers to help you get ready for your adventure:

What time of year is ideal for traveling to Gran Canaria?

Gran Canaria is a well-liked vacation spot all year round due to its pleasant temperature. The ideal time to go, nevertheless, will depend on your interests. Because summer temperatures typically range from 25 to 30°C (77 to 86°F), **June through August are the best months to visit beaches and take advantage of the sun.** Consider going in the spring (**March to May) or autumn (September to November),** when the weather is nicer and lodging may be less expensive if you want fewer people and better weather.

Which attractions in Gran Canaria are the most popular?

A wide variety of attractions may be found in Gran Canaria, such as stunning beaches, historical monuments, natural parks, and cultural icons. The breathtaking dunes of Maspalomas, the scenic town of Puerto de Mogán, the ancient Vegueta neighborhood in Las Palmas, and the untamed landscapes of Roque Nublo and Pico de las Nieves are a few must-see sights.

What is the route to Gran Canaria?

Gran Canaria Airport (LPA), which is about eighteen kilometers south of Las Palmas, the capital, serves Gran Canaria. In addition to connecting flights from other locations, the airport provides direct flights from major cities around Europe. Additionally, travelers from other Canary Islands, such as Tenerife and Fuerteventura, may go by ferry to Gran Canaria.

What means of transportation are there on the island?

The transportation system of Gran Canaria is well-developed and includes ride-sharing services, taxis, buses, and rental automobiles. With lines linking the island's main cities and popular tourist spots, public buses provide an inexpensive means of transportation. While taxis and ride-sharing services are easily accessible for shorter trips, rental automobiles provide flexibility and convenience for visiting more rural places.

What lodging choices are there in Gran Canaria?
There are many different lodging alternatives available in Gran Canaria to fit every taste and budget. Luxurious resorts, boutique hotels, affordable hostels, holiday homes, and even camping and glamping locations are available to visitors. Puerto Rico, Puerto de Mogán, Las Palmas, and Maspalomas are popular places to stay.

Is having travel insurance required while going to Gran Canaria?
Although not required, travel insurance is strongly advised for visitors to Gran Canaria. Travel insurance may give financial security and peace of mind during your vacation by covering medical emergencies, trip cancellations, lost baggage, and other unforeseen incidents.

Do you have any health or safety advice for travelers visiting Gran Canaria?

Although most people find Gran Canaria to be a secure location, it's always advisable to take steps to guarantee a fun and safe journey. To avoid sunburn and dehydration, make sure you drink enough water, use sunscreen, and maintain proper hygiene. Additionally, use caution while swimming in the water since some spots may have strong currents. In case of any unanticipated events, it's also a good idea to get acquainted with the medical facilities and emergency contacts in your area.

Which sights and activities in Gran Canaria are reasonably priced?

For tourists on a limited budget, Gran Canaria has a tonne of affordable sights and activities to choose from. Among the alternatives are taking in the island's natural beauties via activities like mountain hikes and touring the markets and cultural landmarks. Access to many beaches is free, and discounts are often offered for guided tours, museums, and other attractions. Furthermore, eating at neighborhood restaurants and street food vendors may be less expensive than dining at fancy establishments.

Does Gran Canaria host any LGBTQ+ friendly places or events?

Gran Canaria is well-known for its LGBTQ+-friendly environment, with several locations and businesses serving the community. Playa del Inglés' Yumbo Centre is a well-known center for LGBTQ+ entertainment and nightlife, with eateries that serve people of all orientations as well as pubs and clubs. In addition, the island has several LGBTQ+ celebrations and events all year long, including the well-known Maspalomas Pride.

What must be packed for a vacation to Gran Canaria?

Be sure to include necessities like swimwear, comfortable walking shoes, a hat, sunscreen, sunglasses, and lightweight clothes appropriate for warm weather while packing for your vacation to Gran Canaria. Bring a daypack, a reusable water bottle, and hiking boots if you want to explore the island's natural regions.

Remember to include travel documentation, electronic gadgets with chargers, and any essential prescriptions. We want to answer some often-asked questions and provide you with the knowledge you need to make the most of your vacation to Gran Canaria. Do not hesitate to contact the local tourist bureau or look for further help from other sources if you have any more queries or worries.

We wish you a safe journey and hope to see you in Gran Canaria soon!

Printed in Great Britain
by Amazon